THIS B
BELONGS TO...

C000147808

FOREST

Name: Age:

Favourite player:

2018/2019

My Predictions...	Actual...
Forest's final position:	
Forest's top scorer:	
Championship winners:	
Championship top scorer:	
FA Cup winners:	
EFL Cup winners:	

Contributors: Peter Rogers

A TWOCAN PUBLICATION

©2018. Published by twocan under licence from Nottingham Forest FC.

ISBN 978-1-912692-34-7

£9

CONTENTS

SQUAD 2018/19

1 COSTEL PANTILIMON

GOALKEEPER   DOB: 01/02/87   COUNTRY: ROMANIA

A vastly experienced international goalkeeper, Pantilimon was a League Cup winner in 2014 after helping Manchester City defeat Sunderland 3-1 in the Wembley final. After impressing on loan last season, the Romanian agreed a permanent three-year deal at the City Ground ahead of the 2018/19 campaign.

2 HILLAL SOUDANI

FORWARD   DOB: 25/11/87   COUNTRY: ALGERIA

Algerian international Soudani came off the bench with devastating effect to score the only goal of the game as Forest recorded their first win of the 2018/19 season at home to Reading on August 11. He joined from Dinamo Zagreb in June 2018 and represented Algeria in the 2014 World Cup finals in Brazil.

3 TOBIAS FIGUEIREDO

DEFENDER   DOB: 02/02/94   COUNTRY: PORTUGAL

Portugal youth international defender Figueiredo, played a dozen games on loan for Forest last season. A classy central-defender who is comfortable on the ball, he completed a permanent switch to the City Ground in the summer and featured in all of Forest's league games in the opening month of the season.

4 DANNY FOX

DEFENDER   DOB: 29/05/86   COUNTRY: SCOTLAND

Much-travelled defender Fox is now one of the club's longest-serving players having made his Forest debut back in February 2014. Despite being born in England and representing the Three Lions at U21 level, he has won full international honours with Scotland, a country he proudly represents through his grandfather.

5 ADLÈNE GUÉDIOURA

| MIDFIELDER | DOB: 12/11/85 | COUNTRY: ALGERIA |

French-born Algerian international Guedioura brings a wealth of experience to the Forest midfield. Now in his second spell with the club, he has previously played for four other English clubs. The first goal of his second stint at Forest came in the opening home game of the season in a 1-1 draw with West Bromwich Albion.

7 LEWIS GRABBAN

| FORWARD | DOB: 12/01/88 | COUNTRY: ENGLAND |

A real Championship goal-machine, Grabban joined Forest from Bournemouth prior to the 2018/19 season. He has in fact featured in three of the last four Championship Play-Off finals, winning promotion to the Premier League with Norwich City in 2015.

6 JACK COLBACK

| MIDFIELDER | DOB: 24/10/89 | COUNTRY: ENGLAND |

All-action midfielder Colback is currently taking in a second loan spell at the City Ground having initially joined the club in January 2018 from Newcastle United. He has real battling qualities and an impressive range of passing skills. Colback began his career with Sunderland.

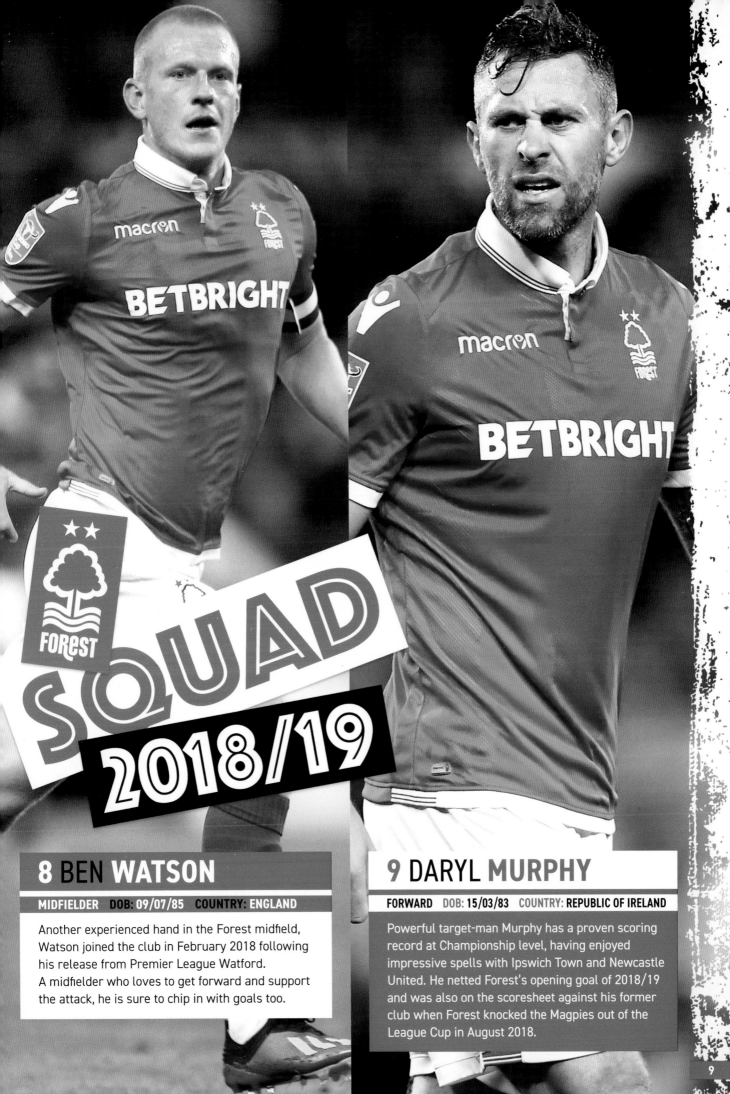

SQUAD 2018/19

8 BEN WATSON

MIDFIELDER   **DOB:** 09/07/85   **COUNTRY: ENGLAND**

Another experienced hand in the Forest midfield, Watson joined the club in February 2018 following his release from Premier League Watford.
A midfielder who loves to get forward and support the attack, he is sure to chip in with goals too.

9 DARYL MURPHY

FORWARD   **DOB:** 15/03/83   **COUNTRY: REPUBLIC OF IRELAND**

Powerful target-man Murphy has a proven scoring record at Championship level, having enjoyed impressive spells with Ipswich Town and Newcastle United. He netted Forest's opening goal of 2018/19 and was also on the scoresheet against his former club when Forest knocked the Magpies out of the League Cup in August 2018.

SQUAD 2018/19

10 JOÃO CARVALHO

MIDFIELDER   **DOB: 09/03/97**   **COUNTRY: PORTUGAL**

Nottingham Forest paid a new club record transfer fee to secure talented Portugal U21 international midfielder Carvalho from Benfica in June 2018. He made his debut in the opening day draw away to Bristol City and adds plenty of creativity to The Reds' forward play.

11 BEN OSBORN

MIDFIELDER   **DOB: 05/08/94**   **COUNTRY: ENGLAND**

Osborn joined the Forest Academy and progressed through the age groups before gaining first-team experience under the management of Stuart Pearce. With the ability to operate at left-back or in a more advanced role his flexibility is one of his many assets.

12 JORDAN SMITH

GOALKEEPER **DOB:** 08/12/94 **COUNTRY:** ENGLAND

A product of the club's Academy, Smith has been with Forest since the age of seven. He made his debut in the 2016/17 season when he came off the bench against Norwich City. Smith has now made over 40 first-team appearances for the club.

14 MATTY CASH

MIDFIELDER **DOB:** 07/08/97 **COUNTRY:** ENGLAND

Attacking midfielder Matty Cash enjoyed an excellent start to the 2018/19 season with four goals in his first six appearances of the season for Aitor Karanka's side. Two of those first four goals of the campaign came in the League Cup, including the vital second goal against Newcastle United.

15 LUKE STEELE

GOALKEEPER **DOB:** 24/09/84 **COUNTRY:** ENGLAND

Capped by England at both U19 and U20 level, goalkeeper Steele was on Manchester United's books in the early part of his career. He joined Forest in August 2018 and made his debut in the League Cup victory at home against Bury later that month.

18 JACK **ROBINSON**

DEFENDER   DOB: 01/09/93   **COUNTRY: ENGLAND**

Former England U21 international defender Robinson began his career with Liverpool. He became the youngest player to represent the Anfield club when he made his debut aged 16 years 250 days old. He joined Forest in June 2018 from QPR and has swiftly settled into his new surroundings at the City Ground.

19 DIOGO **GONÇALVES**

MIDFIELDER   DOB: 06/02/97   **COUNTRY: PORTUGAL**

Portugal U21 international winger Goncalves arrived at the City Ground in June 2018. He joined the club on a season-long loan from Benfica and joined compatriot João Carvalho in switching from the Portuguese side. His Forest debut came on the opening day of the season away to Bristol City.

20 MICHAEL DAWSON

DEFENDER   DOB: 18/11/83   COUNTRY: ENGLAND

In May 2018, Dawson's career went full circle as he returned to Nottingham Forest, having first turned professional at the City Ground back in 2000. A first-class defender who has starred in the Premier League with Tottenham Hotspur and Hull City, he has won four full caps for England.

22 RYAN YATES

MIDFIELDER   DOB: 21/11/97   COUNTRY: ENGLAND

Young midfielder Yates has benefited from valuable loan spells with Barrow, Shrewsbury Town, Notts County and Scunthorpe United. In the summer of 2018, he agreed a new three-year deal with Forest and made his first-team debut in this season's League Cup victory against Bury.

23 JOE LOLLEY

MIDFIELDER   **DOB:** 25/08/92   **COUNTRY:** ENGLAND

After impressing with Huddersfield Town, Joe Lolley joined Nottingham Forest in January 2018. The exciting winger agreed a four-and-a-half-year deal at the City Ground and hit the ground running with his first goal for the club arriving in February's 5-2 romp at QPR.

SQUAD 2018/19

25 SAM BYRAM

DEFENDER   **DOB:** 16/09/93   **COUNTRY:** ENGLAND

Signed on loan from West Ham United for the 2018/19 campaign, right-back Byram brings plenty of Championship experience to the side, having previously played over 100 games for Leeds United at this level. His Forest debut came in the League Cup penalty shoot-out victory against Bury when he was one of the side's successful penalty takers.

26 LIAM BRIDCUTT

MIDFIELDER   **DOB: 08/05/89**   **COUNTRY: SCOTLAND**

Defensive midfielder Bridcutt provides real steel to the Forest side and his skills can help protect the back four. The 29-year-old has great experience following spells with Brighton & Hove Albion, Sunderland and Leeds United. He qualifies to play for Scotland via his Edinburgh-born grandfather and has won two full caps for the Tartan Army.

27 TENDAYI DARIKWA

DEFENDER   **DOB: 13/12/91**   **COUNTRY: ZIMBABWE**

Nottingham-born defender Darikwa has gained international recognition with Zimbabwe due to his Zimbabwean heritage. He began his career with Chesterfield and joined Burnley in 2015, before returning home to the City Ground in July 2017. A regular face in the Forest defence as the 2018/19 season got underway.

43 ARVIN **APPIAH**

FORWARD   **DOB: 05/01/01**   **COUNTRY: ENGLAND**

Highly-rated teenager Appiah looks set to have the raw potential to force his way into Aitor Karanka's first-team plans during the 2018/19 campaign. A product of the club's Academy, Appiah has already featured regularly for the U23 side and has played international football for England at U-17 level.

![SQUAD 2018/19]

31 GIL **DIAS**

FORWARD   **DOB: 28/09/96**   **COUNTRY: PORTUGAL**

Dias makes up the trio of Portuguese players to arrive at the City Ground in the summer of 2018. The skilful winger has joined Forest from Monaco on a season-long loan. He netted his first goal in a Forest shirt when he grabbed the last-gasp third goal in the League Cup victory over Premier League Newcastle in August.

44 MICHAEL **HEFELE**

DEFENDER   **DOB: 01/09/90**   **COUNTRY: GERMANY**

German defender Hefele joined Forest in the summer of 2018 from Premier League Huddersfield Town. A star performer in the Terriers' 2016/17 surprise promotion, Hefele found first-team chances hard to come by at Premier League level and jumped at the chance of a summer switch to the City Ground. Like many summer signings, Hefele made his Forest debut in the League Cup victory against Bury.

Forest Rule!

The Writing's on the Wall...
Decorate this wall and show your love for Forest!

FOREST

ADLENE
GUEDIOURA

Magic MOMENT

45'

★★ FOREST

Champions OF EUROPE

FIXTURE:	European Cup Final
DATE:	Wednesday 30 May 1979
SCORE:	Nottingham Forest 1 Malmo 0
VENUE:	Olympic Stadium, Munich
ATTENDANCE:	68,000

MOLLER 1

FRANCIS 7

ROBERTSON 11

R.ANDERSSON 2

PRYTZ 8

M.ANDERSSON 5

4 JONSSON

ERLANDSSON 3

FRANCIS 7

BOWYER 8

BIRTLES 9

WOODCOCK 10

LJUNGBERG 7

4 McGOVERN

Trevor Francis was Forest's goalscoring hero as Brian Clough's side won the European Cup for the first time in 1979.

Swedish side Malmo were the opposition with the final held in Munich's Olympic Stadium on 30 May 1979.

Malmo were a well-organised and defensively-minded outfit that Clough's men found hard to break down. Despite a first half of almost constant Forest pressure, the game remained goalless as injury time at the end of the opening period began. John Robertson then picked the perfect moment to beat two defenders down the left before whipping in an inviting cross to the far post where Francis was perfectly placed to head home the only goal of the game.

Watch out for these Danger Men when Forest meet their Championship rivals...

DANGER MEN

ASTON VILLA
Jack Grealish

Attacking midfielder Jack Grealish is sure to be the driving force behind Aston Villa once again in 2018/19.

The talented playmaker is a Villa fan and will be going full throttle to help Steve Bruce's side win promotion back to the Premier League. Villa were delighted to keep him at the club following a summer of speculation about the England under-21 star's future.

BOLTON WANDERERS
Yanic Wildschut

Dutch midfielder Yanic Wildschut joined Bolton Wanderers on a season-long loan deal from Championship rivals Norwich City in July 2018.

The talented 27-year-old, who loves to run at the opposition, enjoyed the perfect start to his Bolton career by scoring the winning goal on the opening day of the season away to West Bromwich Albion.

BIRMINGHAM CITY
Che Adams

After joining Blues from Sheffield United in August 2016, all-action midfielder Che Adams wasted little time in showing the St Andrew's faithful just what he was all about.

Adams wrote his name into Birmingham City folklore on the final day of the 2016/17 campaign, scoring the goal that preserved the club's Championship status. He is sure to be a key player for Garry Monk's men in 2018/19.

BRENTFORD
Ollie Watkins

One of the most exciting and talented footballers outside of the Premier League, Ollie Watkins has been a roaring success since joining Brentford from Exeter City in the summer of 2017.

He netted an impressive eleven goals in all competitions in his first season at Griffin Park. He loves to let fly from distance and has scored a number of spectacular goals for the Bees.

BLACKBURN ROVERS
Elliott Bennett

Experienced winger Elliott Bennett played a vital role in Rovers' promotion from League One in 2017/18.

The former Brighton and Norwich man has been a great influence on the younger players at Ewood Park and will be an important member of Tony Mowbray's team once again now they are back in the Championship.

BRISTOL CITY
Andreas Weimann

Much-travelled Austrian striker Andreas Weimann joined Bristol City ahead of the 2018/19 season, agreeing a three-year deal at Ashton Gate.

Weimann is a vastly experienced forward who knows the English game well following spells with Aston Villa, Watford, Derby County and Wolves. The Robins will be looking for Weimann to grab the goals to fire them into Play-Off contention.

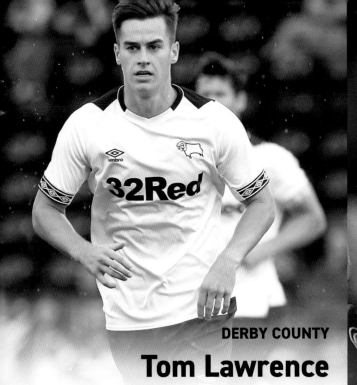

DERBY COUNTY
Tom Lawrence

Wales international midfielder Tom Lawrence, looks set to play a vital role at Pride Park in 2018/19 under new Derby boss Frank Lampard.

The Rams' midfielder certainly has an eye for goal and with Lampard to guide him, Lawrence could well become one of the Championship's star turns over the coming months. He began the season in fine form with two goals in Derby's opening two games.

LEEDS UNITED
Patrick Bamford

A proven goalscorer in the Championship, Patrick Bamford joined Leeds United in the summer of 2018 from Middlesbrough.

Bamford is a great finisher, who also has great awareness of those around him. His arrival at Elland Road has certainly heightened the levels of expectation among the Leeds United fans.

HULL CITY
Fraizer Campbell

Vastly-experienced striker Fraizer Campbell brings an enormous amount of knowhow to the Tigers' front line.

A former England international, Campbell has spent time on the books at some of the country's biggest clubs including Manchester United and Tottenham Hotspur. Now in his second spell with Hull, he was on target against Sheffield Wednesday to ensure the Tigers' first point of the 2018/19 season.

MIDDLESBROUGH
Jonny Howson

An experienced Championship campaigner, Jonny Howson knows exactly what is needed to win promotion from English football's second tier - he was a Play-Off winner with Norwich City in 2015.

With the ability to win possession, pass intelligently and score goals, Howson really is the complete midfielder. He joined Boro in the summer of 2017 and helped the Riverside club to the Play-Off semi-finals last season and will be looking to help Boro return to the Premier League in 2019.

IPSWICH TOWN
Jon Nolan

Talented midfielder Jon Nolan was an instrumental player for Shrewsbury Town in 2017/18 as the Shrews reached both the Checkatrade Trophy final and the League One Play-Off final.

In August 2018, he joined Ipswich Town and reunited with his former Shrewsbury boss Paul Hurst who took over at Portman Road three months earlier. Nolan is expected to flourish at Championship level.

MILLWALL
Steve Morison

Evergreen forward Steve Morison is currently enjoying his second spell with the Lions.

His goals helped propel the South London club to the verge of the Play-Offs last season. Approaching 300 games for Millwall and almost 100 goals, Morison is a vital member of Neil Harris' squad with a positive influence both on and off the pitch.

Watch out for these Danger Men when Forest meet their Championship rivals...

DANGER MEN

QUEENS PARK RANGERS

Eberechi Eze

After spending a loan spell with Wycombe Wanderers last season, Eze has returned to Loftus Road and cemented himself a place in the heart of the Hoops' midfield.

A true box-to-box midfielder, Eze loves to plough forward and lend his support to attacking situations. The 20-year-old produced a number of eye-catching displays at the start of the 2018/19 season and was on target in Rangers' first home game of the season against Sheffield United.

NORWICH CITY

Jordan Rhodes

Signed on loan from Sheffield Wednesday, the Canaries will be hopeful that striker Jordan Rhodes can rediscover his goalscoring form during the 2018/19 season at Carrow Road.

A prolific marksman with Huddersfield Town and Blackburn Rovers, Rhodes marked his Carrow Road debut with a goal during a thrilling seven-goal clash with West Bromwich Albion.

READING

Jon Dadi Bodvarsson

Icelandic international forward Jon Dadi Bodvarsson has become something of a cult hero with Reading fans at the Madejski Stadium after netting ten goals for the Royals last season.

He represented his country at the 2018 World Cup finals in Russia and also netted Reading's first goal of the new 2018/19 campaign.

PRESTON NORTH END

Tom Barkhuizen

After beginning his career with Preston's rivals Blackpool, striker Tom Barkhuizen is a player who will be looking to make his mark for Alex Neil's side in 2018/19.

A string of loan spells with Hereford United, Fleetwood Town and Morecambe resulted in a permanent switch to Morecambe and it was his goalscoring form at the Globe Arena that alerted North End who signed him in November 2016.

ROTHERHAM UNITED

Joe Newell

Versatile midfielder Joe Newell was one of the Millers' heroes as Rotherham United won promotion to the Championship via the League One Play-Offs.

With the ability to operate in a creative central midfield berth or out on the wing, Newell was almost ever-present for the Millers last season and will be a key performer for Paul Warne's men in their 2018/19 Championship campaign.

SHEFFIELD UNITED
Billy Sharp

Now in his third spell with the Blades, and still looking as lively as ever in front of goal, Billy Sharp will once again be at the forefront of manager Chris Wilder's thoughts at Bramall Lane

Sharp became the Sheffield United captain in 2016 and is now closing in on 200 goals for the club.

SWANSEA CITY
Oliver McBurnie

Following a highly productive loan spell in the Championship with Barnsley in the second-half of last season, Oliver McBurnie has earned the chance to lead the line for Swansea City as the Welsh club bid to bounce back to the top-flight in 2018/19.

McBurnie scored nine goals in 17 outings for a struggling Tykes team last season and will now look to grab his Swansea opportunity with both hands.

SHEFFIELD WEDNESDAY
Fernando Forestieri

The jewel in Sheffield Wednesday's crown, all eyes at Hillsborough will once again be on skilful Italian Fernando Forestieri who is the man that makes the Owls tick.

The Wednesday fans will be looking for Forestieri to inspire those around him as the club searches for an improved season under Jos Luhakay.

WEST BROMWICH ALBION
Jay Rodriguez

Burnley-born England striker Jay Rodriguez began his career at his hometown club before moving on to the Premier League with Southampton and then West Bromwich Albion.

A cool customer with the ball at his feet, Rodriguez has all the skills to really shine in the Championship for an Albion side who will hope their stay in the second-tier is a brief one.

STOKE CITY
Benik Afobe

Striker Benik Afobe is the man charged with scoring the goals to fire Stoke City back to the Premier League at the first time of asking.

Afobe joined the Potters on loan from Wolverhampton Wanderers in June 2018 and his physical presence and goal threat are sure to play a huge part in the Potters' 2018/19 promotion push.

WIGAN ATHLETIC
Nick Powell

Midfielder Nick Powell was nominated for the EFL League One Player of the Season award after an outstanding season in the Latics' 2017/18 title-winning campaign.

A technically gifted player with the ability to score goals and create chances for others, Powell will certainly be one of the first names on Paul Cook's teamsheet as Wigan look to establish themselves at Championship level.

A real fans favourite at the City Ground, Stuart Pearce played a staggering 524 games for Forest and hammered home an incredible 89 goals from the left-back berth during an unforgettable 12-year spell with the club.

Pearce was recruited from Coventry City by legendry Forest boss Brian Clough in 1985 and went on to taste domestic success at club level while also proceeding to make the England left-back shirt his own.

Pearce ended his Forest playing career in 1997 and returned to the City Ground as manager in July 2014. Although his time in charge was not the success everyone at the club hoped for, he remains a true Nottingham Forest giant.

BORN:

STUART PEARCE
22 APRIL 1962 · HAMMERSMITH, LONDON

POSITION:

LEFT-BACK

FOREST DEBUT:

LUTON TOWN 1-1 NOTTINGHAM FOREST
DIVISION ONE
17 AUGUST 1985

STAT ATTACK
STUART PEARCE

FOREST APPEARANCES:

APPEARANCES	LEAGUE	FA CUP	LEAGUE CUP	OTHERS
524	402	38	60	24

FOREST GOALS:

GOALS	LEAGUE	FA CUP	LEAGUE CUP	OTHERS
89	63	10	10	6

ENGLAND INTERNATIONAL:

APPEARANCES	GOALS
78	5

INTERNATIONAL DEBUT:

ENGLAND 1-1 BRAZIL
19 MAY 1987

MATTY
CASH

FAN'TASTIC

There are five Forest legends hiding in the crowd...
Can you spot them?

DARYL
MURPHY

**Have fun colouring
this picture of Gil Dias...**

FOREST

GIL
DIAS

Magic MOMENT

87'

BATTLE OF *Britain*

FIXTURE: European Cup First Round First Leg

DATE: Wednesday 13 September 1978

SCORE: Nottingham Forest 2 Liverpool 0

VENUE: City Ground

ATTENDANCE: 38,316

After pipping Liverpool to the First Division title only four months earlier, Nottingham Forest were then paired with the men from Anfield in an all-British European Cup first round tie in September 1978.

On a truly memorable night at the City Ground, Forest lead through a first-half goal from Gary Birtles, but as the clock ticked closer to the 90-minute mark, the Forest faithful were wondering if one goal would be enough ahead of a tricky second leg at Anfield.

With three minutes remaining, Brian Clough's men made it two as full-back Colin Barrett hammered home one of the City Ground's most memorable goals.

Birtles crossed from the left and Tony Woodcock cushioned the ball back to the edge of the six-yard box where Barrett was on hand to ram the ball past Ray Clemence.

The second leg ended goalless and Forest progressed to the second round and ultimately European glory in the final.

PLAYER OF THE SEASON

BEN OSBORN

A proud graduate of the Nottingham Forest academy system, Ben Osborn achieved another personal accolade as he was named the 2017/18 Player of the Season following a fans' vote.

Having made his debut for the club in a 1-1 draw at Ipswich Town in March 2014, Osborn never looked back and has now made almost 200 appearances for the club, despite not having yet spent five years in the first team.

One of Osborn's most memorable moments for Forest came in his first full season for the club when he scored the famous last-minute winner against Derby County in the East Midlands derby at Pride Park - a goal that will forever go down in Forest folklore.

It says something that Osborn has been picked regularly by every manager that has taken charge of the club as they cite his non-stop running and energy as one of the key components in their respective teams.

In the 2017/18 season, Osborn made an impressive 51 appearances for The Reds and scored four times, including a superb strike in the 2-0 win over eventual champions Wolverhampton Wanderers at Molineux back in January.

In recent times, Osborn's versatility and willingness to help the team has seen him play in a number of different positions including just behind the striker, in central midfield and at left-back and his exceptional work-rate has made him one of the first names on the teamsheet.

The 24-year-old continues to be an important part of the Forest squad and he is a big favourite with The Reds' supporters due to his unselfish nature and willingness to work harder for the team than anyone else.

ERIC LICHAJ

FOREST 4-2 ARSENAL
EMIRATES FA CUP THIRD ROUND

The most memorable goal came in the most memorable game of the season as Eric Lichaj's incredible strike helped Forest to knock FA Cup holders Arsenal out of the competition.

The Reds had taken an early lead through Lichaj's first goal of the night and although that was cancelled out by a close-range finish from Per Mertesacker, the American was not about to let the headlines be taken away from him.

Matty Cash raced down the right-hand channel and delivered a cross into the Arsenal 18-yard box which the Gunners could only head as far out as the edge of the penalty area.

Lichaj brought the ball down on his chest and fired a stunning right-footed volley beyond David Ospina and into the top corner of the net. The City Ground erupted in celebration as Lichaj wheeled away to celebrate in front of the A Block.

Two second-half penalties from Ben Brereton and Kieran Dowell helped The Reds to secure a memorable 4-2 win over Arsene Wenger's side despite a late consolation strike from Danny Welbeck, but the night will long be remembered for Lichaj's incredible effort.

Lichaj's two goals on the night also earned another souvenir as he became the proud owner of a new dog which he appropriately named 'Gunner'. His wife Kathryn had said he would be allowed to get a dog when he scored a hat-trick and although he only scored twice, an internet campaign from Forest fans persuaded her to add a new member to the family.

So, it turns out that every dog does indeed have its day!

GOAL
OF THE SEASON

GUESS THE CLUB

Can you work out which European Club each set of clues is pointing to?

1 ANSWER

3 ANSWER

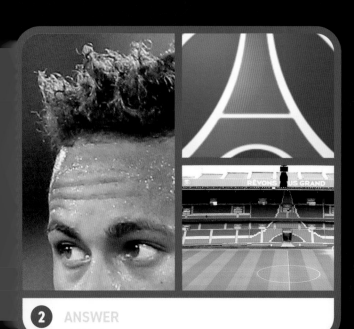

2 ANSWER

4 ANSWER

5 ANSWER

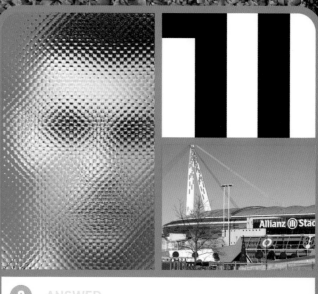

8 ANSWER

6 ANSWER

9 ANSWER

7 ANSWER

10 ANSWER

LOCAL HEROES

The East Midlands derby between Nottingham Forest and Derby County is one of the biggest and most historic rivalries in English football and there have been some classic encounters down the years.

A large number of players and managers have represented both clubs, including the legendary Brian Clough, and the rivalry continues to run as deeply as it ever has.

Here we take a look at three of Forest's best victories over the men from down the A52...

DERBY 1
FOREST 2

SATURDAY 17 JANUARY 2015

Forest went into the East Midlands derby at Pride Park in wretched form but then delivered one of the most memorable results in the club's recent history.

The Reds had trailed to an early own goal from Henri Lansbury, but Britt Assombalonga stabbed the ball home with 15 minutes to play to level the scores and seemingly earn Forest a share of the points.

However, with almost the last kick of the game, Ben Osborn strode through the middle third and fired a stunning effort beyond Lee Grant to spark scenes of wild celebration in the away end and give manager Stuart Pearce a memorable East Midlands derby victory.

FOREST 5-2 DERBY

WEDNESDAY 29 DECEMBER 2010

On a misty night on Trentside, Forest turned in a terrific performance to cruise to a 5-2 victory over their near-neighbours and keep up their unbeaten home run.

Luke Chambers opened the scoring after only two minutes when he headed home from close range and despite Luke Moore equalising soon after, Forest grabbed the advantage back again when Marcus Tudgay netted against his former club.

Tudgay's second goal of the night handed Forest a two-goal lead at the break and they extended that advantage after half-time when another former Derby man, Robert Earnshaw, fired home a fourth goal.

Kris Commons, formerly of Forest, reduced the arrears when his low free-kick deflected into the net, but the Reds had the last word on a memorable night when Earnshaw rocketed a shot into the bottom corner to put gloss on the scoreline.

FOREST 3-0 DERBY

SATURDAY 27 AUGUST 1977

Forest were newcomers to the First Division in the 1977/78 season, but having started the campaign with wins over Everton and Bristol City, confidence was high in the Reds' camp ahead of the visit of their biggest rivals.

Peter Withe lashed home his first goal of the afternoon on 31 minutes before he scored his fourth in three games to double the lead midway through the second half and put the Reds in command of the contest.

The three points were firmly secured with 12 minutes to play when John Robertson produced a fine finish which ensured Forest claimed the bragging rights and stayed at the top of the First Division table with their 100% record intact.

Striker Stan Collymore displayed sensational goalscoring form over a two-year City Ground career under the management of Frank Clark.

After rising to fame with an impressive goals-to-games ratio during his Southend United career, Collymore joined Forest in the summer of 1993 for a £2M transfer fee. He hit the ground running and his goals helped the team's march up the table as Forest secured automatic promotion and an immediate return to the Premier League.

If his first season at Forest was impressive, then his second was outstanding - Collymore hammered home 22 Premier League goals as Forest finished third in the top-flight. His form subsequently led to Liverpool paying a then British record transfer fee of £8.5M for him in the summer of 1995.

BORN:

STANLEY VICTOR COLLYMORE
22 JANUARY 1971 · CANNOCK, STAFFORDSHIRE

POSITION:

STRIKER

FOREST DEBUT:

CRYSTAL PALACE 2-0 NOTTINGHAM FOREST
FIRST DIVISION
24 AUGUST 1993

STAT ATTACK
STAN COLLYMORE

FOREST APPEARANCES:

APPEARANCES	LEAGUE	FA CUP	LEAGUE CUP	OTHERS
78	65	2	9	2

FOREST GOALS:

GOALS	LEAGUE	FA CUP	LEAGUE CUP	OTHERS
45	41	1	2	1

ENGLAND INTERNATIONAL:

APPEARANCES	GOALS
3	0

INTERNATIONAL DEBUT:

ENGLAND 2-1 JAPAN
3 JUNE 1995

FOREST

BEN
WATSON

1

2

3

4

5

...and the three here?

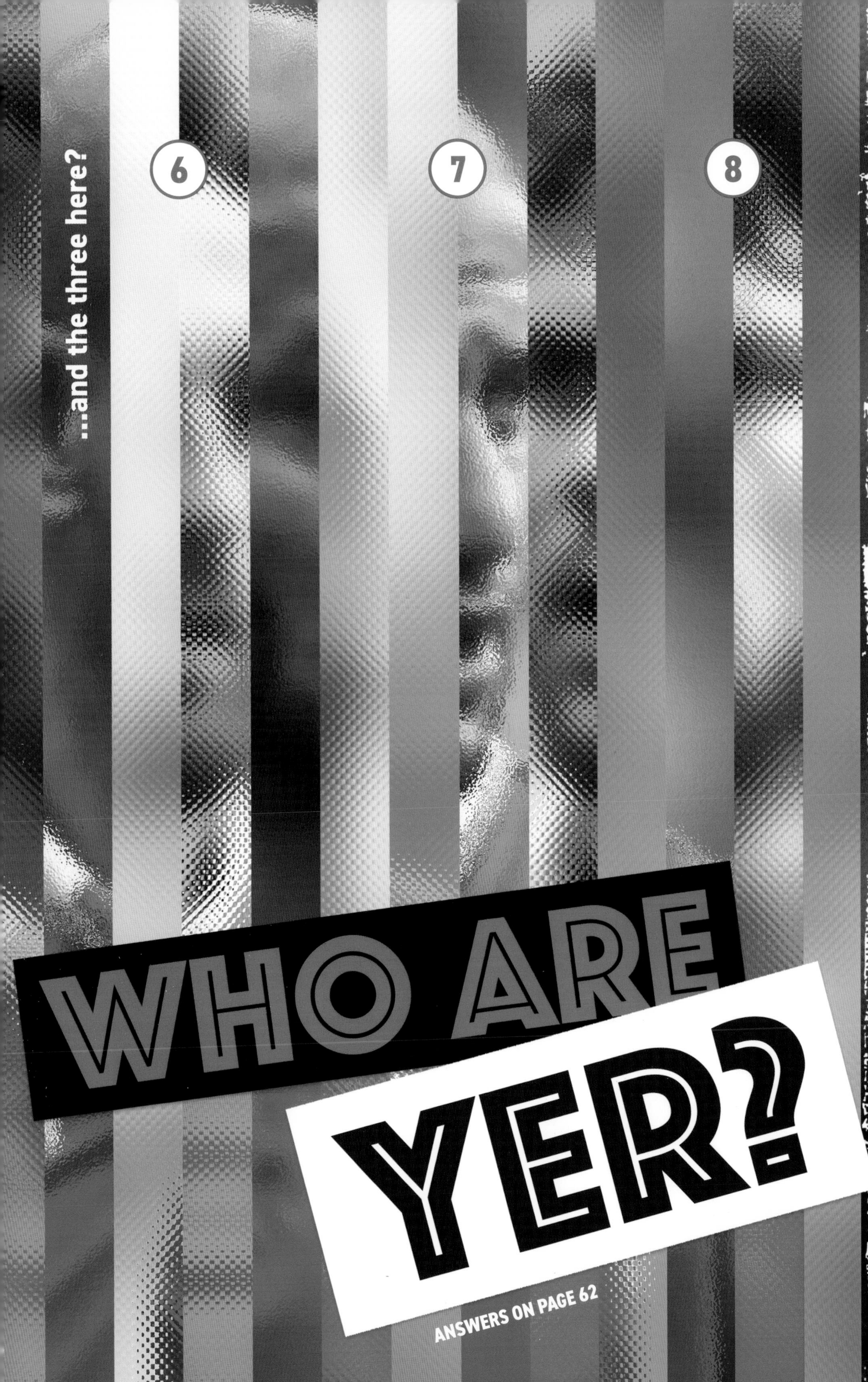

6

7

8

WHO ARE YER?

ANSWERS ON PAGE 62

CARVALHO

Can you find the eight differences between these celebration photos?

SPOT THE DIFFERENCE

ANSWERS ON PAGE 62

FOREST 4
ARSENAL 2

EMIRATES FA CUP
THIRD ROUND
SUNDAY 7 JANUARY 2018

Emirates FA Cup holders Arsenal were dispatched on a memorable afternoon at The City Ground as The Reds dumped Arsene Wenger's side out of the competition.

An unexpected brace from full-back Eric Lichaj - including a superb volley - put Forest 2-1 up at half-time after German defender Per Mertesacker had levelled the scores.

Forest took control of the game in the second half as Ben Brereton stepped up to confidently stroke home a penalty just after the hour mark, but England international Danny Welbeck reduced the deficit for The Gunners with ten minutes to play.

However, another spot kick, this time converted by Kieran Dowell secured a famous victory in front of a packed crowd on Trentside.

WOLVES 0-2 FOREST

SKY BET CHAMPIONSHIP
SATURDAY 20 JANUARY 2018

In Aitor Karanka's second game as Forest manager, The Reds visited runaway league leaders Wolves and produced a stunning display to upset the odds and come away with three points.

Brilliant from start to finish, Forest were on top for most of the first half and deservedly took the lead on 40 minutes as Kieran Dowell's deflected strike found the back of the net. Three minutes later and The Reds had the crucial second goal as Ben Osborn lashed an effort into the top corner following fine work from Matty Cash to give them a well-deserved half-time lead.

A solid defensive display in the second period kept Wolves at arm's length and ensured The Reds left Molineux with the victory.

QPR 2-5 FOREST

SKY BET CHAMPIONSHIP
SATURDAY 24 FEBRUARY 2018

A breath-taking display of attacking football saw Forest run riot in West London as they defeated QPR 5-2 at Loftus Road.

Loanee Lee Tomlin put Forest in front with a fine finish high into the net, and he doubled his and Forest's tally shortly after half-time with a superb curling shot. Joe Lolley lashed an effort into the bottom corner to make it 3-0 with his first goal for the club, before a flurry of goals in the final 20 minutes.

Massimo Luongo pulled a goal back for Rangers then Matty Cash fired home from a tight angle to make it 4-1. Two minutes later and Matt Smith had reduced the arrears, before the scoring was rounded off with a solo effort by Ben Brereton to add the gloss to a great away victory.

1 Who scored Forest's first League goal last season?

ANSWER

WCASTLE UNIT

ANSWER

2 What was the score when Forest knocked the Magpies out of the League Cup?

3 Who top scored last season with nine league goals?

ANSWER

4 Last season, Forest's highest goalscoring performance was against which team and what was the score?

ANSWER

5 How many clean sheets did Forest keep in the League in 2017/18?

ANSWER

ANSWER

6 Which player made the most League appearances in 2017/18 with 46?

2017/18
END OF TERM
EXAM

How much did you learn about the Forest's last campaign?

7 Who was Forest' first win of the 2017/18 season against?

ANSWER

8 Which Forest player received the most yellow cards in the League last season?

ANSWER

9 Who scored the goals when Forest beat Burton Albion 2-0 at the City Ground

ANSWER

10 How many goals did Forest score in the League last season?

ANSWER

FAST FORWARD>>

FOREST V LEEDS UNITED

SKY BET CHAMPIONSHIP
TUESDAY 1 JANUARY 2019

Nottingham Forest kick-off 2019 with the visit of Leeds United to The City Ground on New Year's Day.

Marcelo Bielsa's side have been hotly-tipped for promotion back to the Premier League this season and made a fine start to the campaign, so this fixture is one not to be missed.

Their visit to Trentside is often one of the most eagerly-anticipated fixtures of the season due to the history between the two clubs, and this match is set to be no different with both sides aiming to be in and around the promotion picture come May.

FOREST V DERBY COUNTY

SKY BET CHAMPIONSHIP
SATURDAY 23 FEBRUARY 2019

The East Midlands derby is the hottest ticket in town every season and this one is no different as Frank Lampard's Rams visit The City Ground in mid-February.

The intense rivalry often delivers drama, excitement and top-draw action and the clash on Trentside is set to be no different. With the reverse fixture played in December at the end of 2018, this game will offer both sides the chance for redemption or an opportunity to steal all the glory by completing a league double.

The last two outings between the two sides at The City Ground have ended in a stalemate so Aitor Karanka will be hoping to get all three points and give Forest fans the bragging rights.

FOREST V BOLTON WANDERERS

SKY BET CHAMPIONSHIP
SUNDAY 5 MAY 2019

Nottingham Forest end the season at home against Bolton Wanderers and will be hoping to have something to celebrate as the curtain falls at The City Ground.

Forest ended last season against the same opposition, with Bolton snatching a late victory at the Macron Stadium to ensure they survived in the Championship, and The Reds will no doubt be looking to get their own back for that result when The Trotters are the visitors in May.

Phil Parkinson's team will be looking to be well clear of any relegation threat this time around, while Aitor Karanka's men will be hoping to end the season in style with a victory against Bolton.

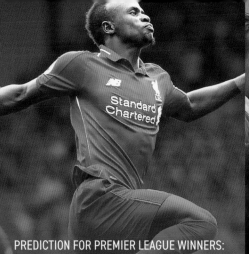

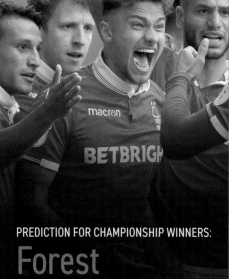

PREDICTION FOR PREMIER LEAGUE WINNERS:
Liverpool

YOUR
PREDICTION:

PREDICTION FOR CHAMPIONSHIP WINNERS:
Forest

YOUR
PREDICTION:

PREDICTION FOR FA CUP WINNERS:
Arsenal

YOUR
PREDICTION:

2018/19
PREDICTIONS

PREDICTION FOR PREMIER LEAGUE
RUNNERS-UP:
Manchester City

YOUR
PREDICTION:

PREDICTION FOR CHAMPIONSHIP
RUNNERS-UP:
Swansea City

YOUR
PREDICTION:

**Here are our
predictions for
the 2018/19
season...**

**What do you
think will happen?**

PREDICTION FOR PREMIER LEAGUE
TOP SCORER:
Harry Kane

YOUR
PREDICTION:

PREDICTION FOR CHAMPIONSHIP
TOP SCORER:
Daryl Murphy

YOUR
PREDICTION:

PREDICTION FOR LEAGUE CUP
WINNERS:
Burnley

YOUR
PREDICTION:

DESIGN YOUR FOREST FOOTY BOOTS

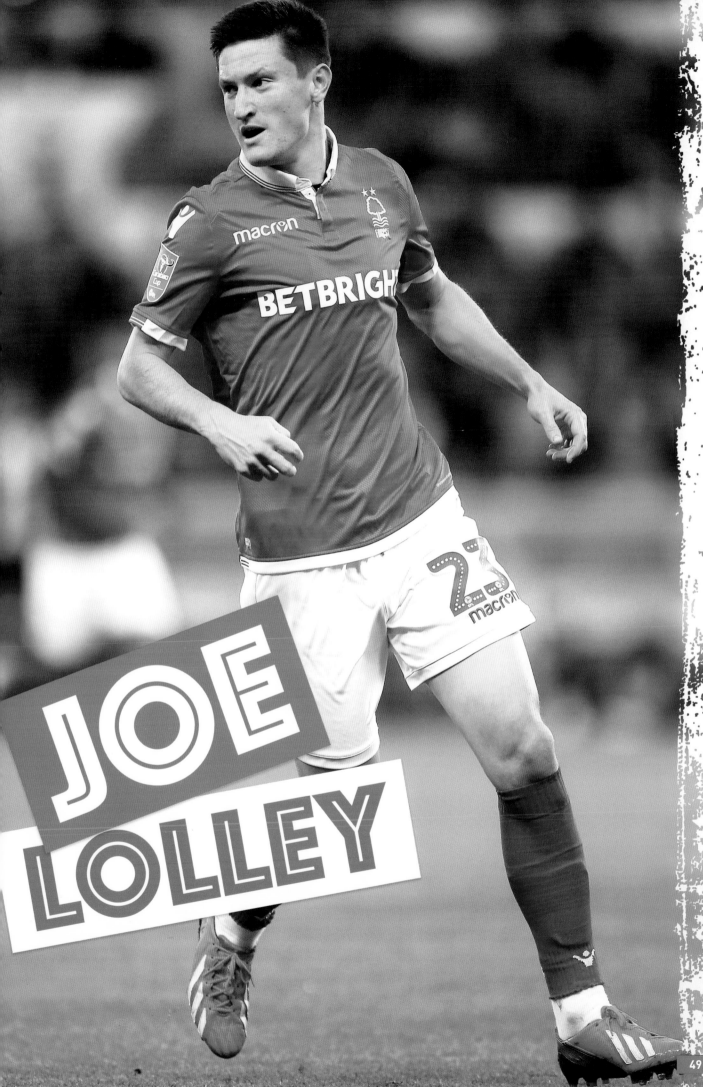

JOE
LOLLEY

BRIAN CLOUGH

Forest have been blessed with a host of great managers down the years - here we take a brief look at two of our finest.

Simply the greatest Nottingham Forest manager of all time, Brian Clough arrived at the City Ground in 1975 and proceeded to oversee the most successful era in the club's history.

Having already enjoyed outstanding success with rivals Derby County, Clough had also managed Brighton & Hove Albion and had an ill-fated 44 days in charge of Leeds United before he succeeded Allan Brown as Forest boss.

The club were 13th in the Second Division when Clough arrived. His decision to reunite with Peter Taylor, who had been with him at Derby, proved a master stroke. The team won promotion from the Second Division in 1976/77 and 12 months later they were incredibly crowned First Division champions!

The club also won the European Cup in back-to-back seasons in 1978/79 and 1979/80 under Clough's guidance.

Remarkably, Clough's unique management style also produced four League Cup triumphs, a Charity Shield win, two successful Full Members Cup campaigns and an FA Cup final appearance in 1991.

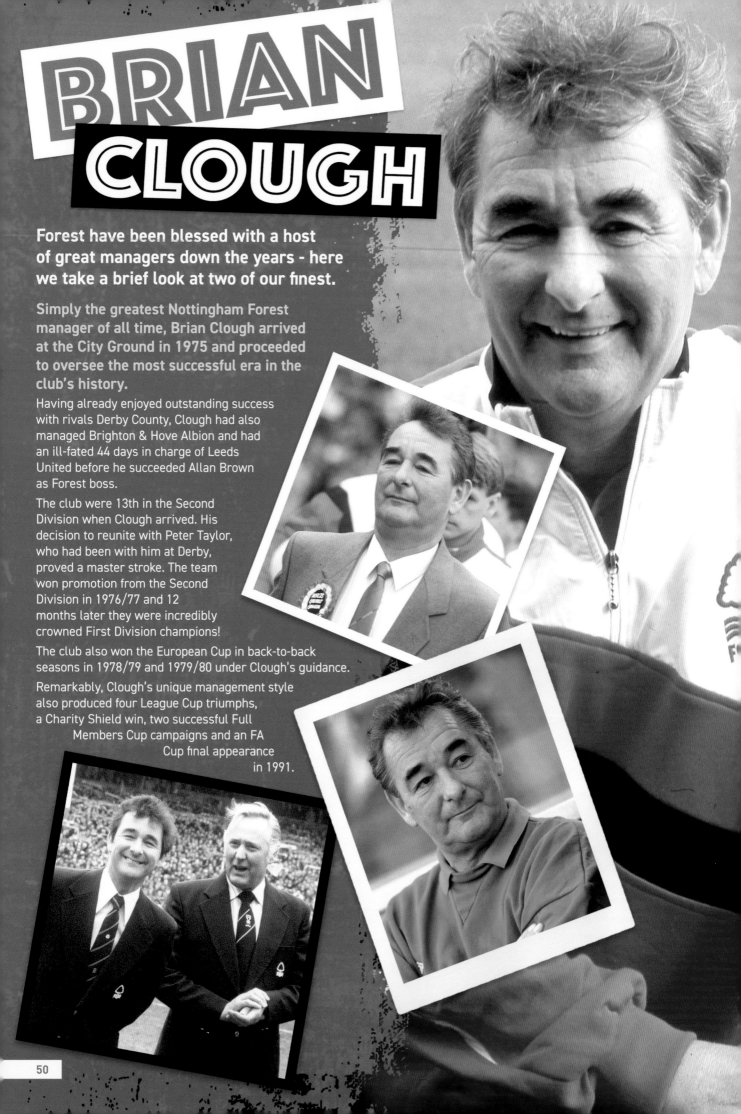

FRANK CLARK

Having enjoyed a trophy-laden playing career with Forest, Frank Clark was a popular choice when he took over from the legendary Brian Clough in 1993.

Having won the First Division title, two League Cups and the European Cup with Forest in the late 1970s, Clark took his first steps in management with Leyton Orient.

Following the club's relegation from the Premier League at the end of the 1992/93 campaign, Clark was charged with guiding Forest back to the top-flight. Following Clough was always going to be a tough role for whoever took up the challenge, but Clark did a remarkable job in securing promotion back to the Premier League at the first time of asking in 1993/94.

Forest secured automatic promotion as Division One runners-up, behind champions Crystal Palace.

In their first season back in the top-flight, Forest achieved a remarkable third-place finish under Clark in 1994/95 and then reached the UEFA Cup quarter-finals the following season.

GREAT GAFFERS

51

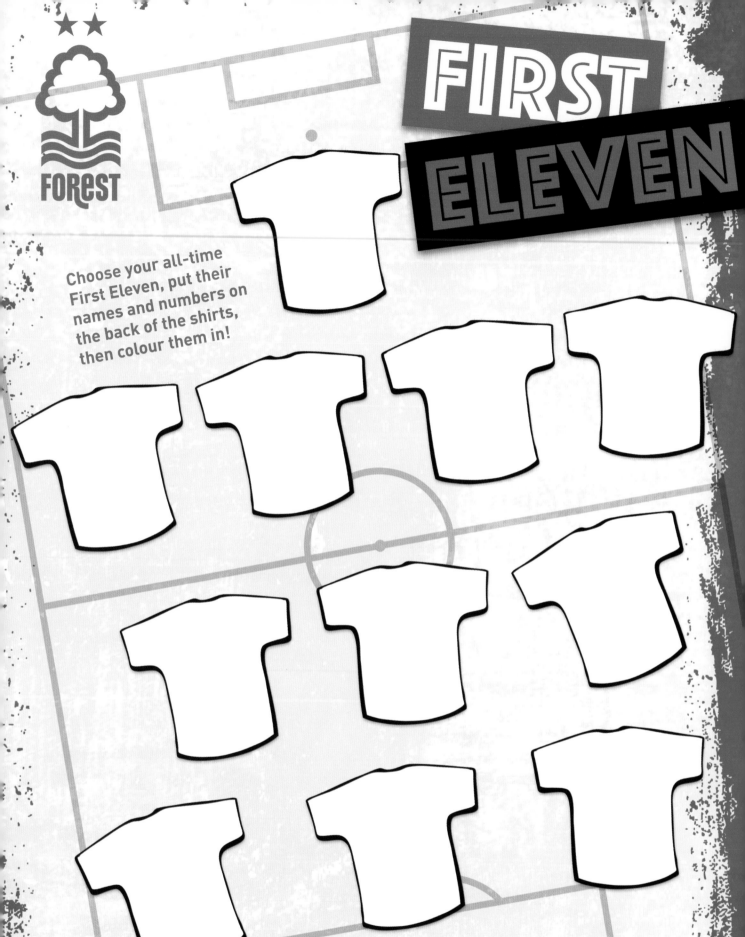

FOREST

FIRST ELEVEN

Choose your all-time First Eleven, put their names and numbers on the back of the shirts, then colour them in!

SPOT THE BALL

The ball is missing from this photo, where should it be?

WHAT BALL?

Can you figure out which is the real ball in this photo?

ANSWERS ON PAGE 62

FOREST

TOBIAS
FIGUEIREDO

Magic MOMENT

90'+2

FOREST

Bragging RIGHTS

FIXTURE:	Sky Bet Championship
DATE:	Saturday 17 January 2015
SCORE:	Derby County 1 Nottingham Forest 2
VENUE:	Pride Park
ATTENDANCE:	32,704

Ben Osborn struck a superb injury-time winner as Nottingham Forest secured local bragging rights with a 2-1 win away to bitter rivals Derby County in January 2015.

Forest had trailed from as early as the 16th minute when Henri Lansbury headed Johnny Russell's first-half corner into his own net. Britt Assombalonga levelled for Forest 15 minutes from time to tee-up a frantic finale as both side went all out for victory.

It was Forest who made the most of their new-found impetus in the final stages when Osborn crashed the ball beyond goalkeeper Lee Grant in time added on. The goal sparked scenes of joy among the travelling fans who tasted sweet revenge for the 5-0 mauling they had suffered at Pride Park the previous season.

HERO HUNT

Here is a list of 20 Forest heroes. All but one of their surnames
are hidden in the grid, can you work out who is missing?

```
W B E A N C H E T T L E J V D B H J G K F M
L M P G A R K T U W J C W E V H G U O L C D
E B U R N S U Z Y E Y A S A O Q A B E G S L
A B D V K A E R Z V H U W H I M Q I O X T N
V N X G M C G Y H R L N C I M B G V S M E A
A Q F J B H T R T G Y S U P O Q E N F C I P
U N R C O D L T O I A O M O J R R P K S D G
C I D S F B E X P M O K U N N F Z A P H R T
J Q P E W I O F O D R I N T L L U O R I X S
L W R M R M W H S S G S B R P V A U O L L W
E U S K E S T O R E Y M O O R E J Y H T I Z
E O N N Y T O S D A J F A B B K A L S O O U
R B Z B A V H N F F A V E E C V Y C N N Y S
O Y S U H T D V I G B H S R O E Q L E D E D
M C A R X G S S R M A D M T W N M I M H O I
Y U B K C T E Y C U N U R S A B L E P F W O
L Z J I R X M K N G A M N O E L Z G Q I B Y
L T S T N R I W Y I H U N N S J E F I O G E
O X A T D N H D A B V J A O E B B P W H K L
C F L K L M G C J L U E I O K A D Y A T E S
K A E A E D I L Q Y K Z I O K C E R X F P S
W Y Y F Q B C O J V U E H S L R N P T O L O
U R E L I P N R W O E C R A E P G J E W L R
K O J P O K V M T Y P L L W U R T T K Y X C
```

Viv **Anderson**	Nigel **Clough**	John **McGovern**	John **Robertson**
Ian **Bowyer**	Stan **Collymore**	Bob **McKinlay**	Peter **Shilton**
Jack **Burkitt**	Mark **Crossley**	Wes **Morgan**	Ian **Storey-Moore**
Kenny **Burns**	Trevor **Francis**	Martin **O'Neill**	Geoff **Thomas**
Steve **Chettle**	Roy **Keane**	Stuart **Pearce**	Des **Walker**

ANSWERS ON PAGE 62

SHIRT SHUFFLE

Here are the away shirts of twelve Premier League and Championship clubs, but their team names have been jumbled up!

Can you figure out who's who?

1. RLVOELPOI
2. ALUMHF
3. FEEHFLDIS NIEUDT
4. RNGBIHMMIA TIYC
5. TEWS AMH DUTNIE
6. YCTSLRA LAPEAC
7. OONEUMTBRUH
8. NQESEU RKAP GRARNES
9. KOETS TCIY
10. WESATNELC TUNEDI
11. ROTPENS HRTNO NDE
12. NATOS LAVIL

Widely regarded as the finest Nottingham Forest player of all time, Scottish international midfielder John Robertson was a star performer in Brian Clough's formidable side that were twice crowned European champions.

The skilful left-winger was one of the first names on Clough's teamsheet and played an incredible 243 consecutive games in a four-year spell between December 1976 and December 1980. After helping Forest win promotion from the Second Division in 1976/77, Robertson netted the winning goal from the penalty spot in the 1978 League Cup Final Replay as Forest lifted the trophy following a 1-0 victory over Liverpool at Old Trafford.

The League Cup win spurred Robertson and his teammates on to even greater achievements. In 1977/78, and against all odds, they lifted the First Division title in their first season back in the top flight. Robertson ended the campaign as the side's ever-present top scorer with 12 league goals and a host of assists for centre-forwards Peter Withe and Tony Woodcock. After becoming a First Division champion in 1977/78, Robertson starred in both of Forest's European Cup triumphs of 1979 and 1980. He provided the cross for Trevor Francis' winning goal in the 1-0 win over Malmo in 1979 and then proceeded to be the hero of the hour himself when he scored the only goal of the game in the 1980 final against Hamburg.

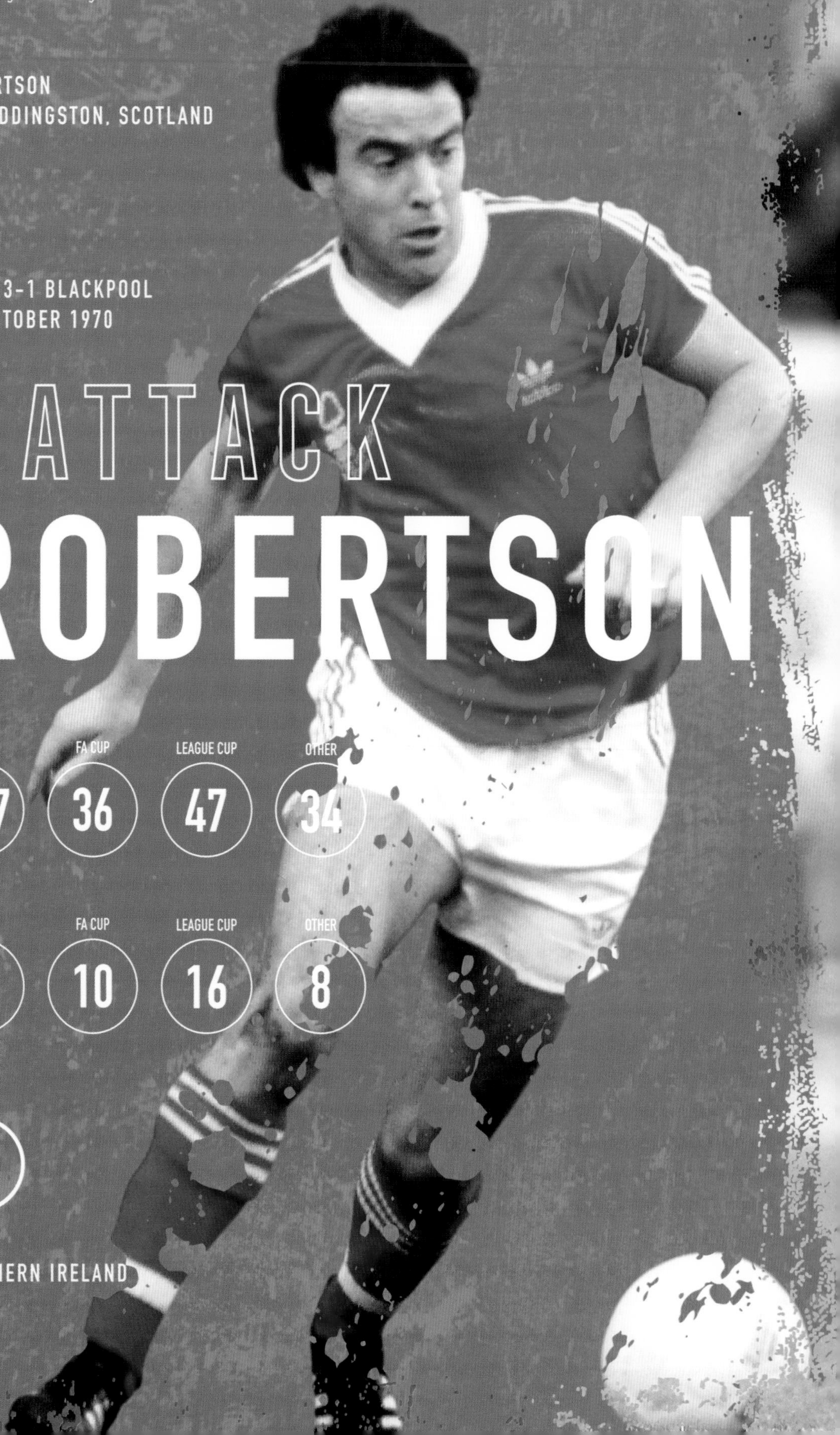

BORN:

JOHN NEILSON ROBERTSON
20 JANUARY 1953 · UDDINGSTON, SCOTLAND

POSITION:

LEFT-WINGER

FOREST DEBUT:

NOTTINGHAM FOREST 3-1 BLACKPOOL
DIVISION ONE · 10 OCTOBER 1970

STAT ATTACK
JOHN ROBERTSON

FOREST APPEARANCES:

APPEARANCES	LEAGUE	FA CUP	LEAGUE CUP	OTHER
514	397	36	47	34

FOREST GOALS:

GOALS	LEAGUE	FA CUP	LEAGUE CUP	OTHER
95	61	10	16	8

SCOTLAND INTERNATIONAL:

APPEARANCES	GOALS
28	8

INTERNATIONAL DEBUT:

SCOTLAND 1-1 NORTHERN IRELAND
13 MAY 1978

DANNY
FOX

How's your knowledge of the laws of the game?

You think you can do better than the man in the middle? here's you chance to prove it...

HEY REF!

1. Daryl Murphy shoots for goal from 25 yards. His fierce drive deflects off your head, wrong-footing the keeper, on its way into the back of the net. What's your call?

A: You award an indirect free-kick to the opposition.

B: It's a goal!

C: You give a drop-ball from where you were hit by the ball.

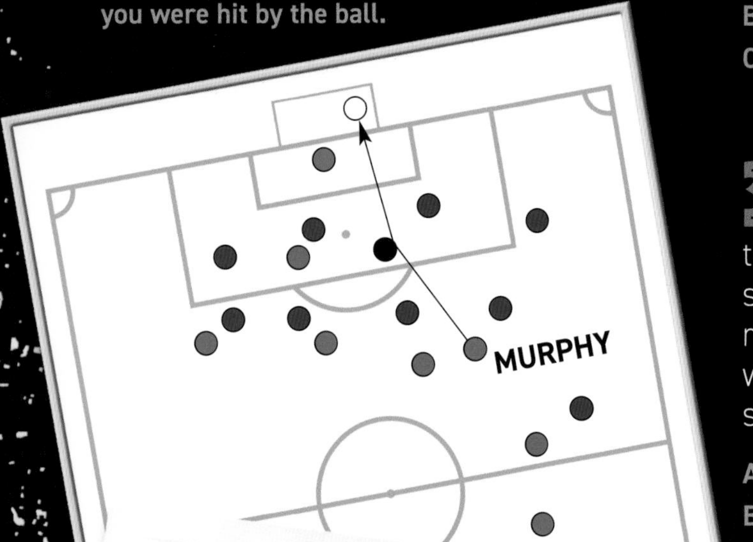

2. Lewis Grabban strikes for goal from six yards, but as he shoots, the ball bursts and stops just before the goal line. Alert, he follows up and taps the ball home. What's your call?

A: It's a goal!

B: You award a penalty kick to Forest.

C: No goal and you restart with a drop ball where the ball burst.

3. Ben Osborn sends the keeper the wrong way from the penalty spot, but his effort hits the post and rebounds straight to Jack Colback who rifles the ball into the net to score. What is your decision?

A: It's a goal!

B: The spot kick has to be retaken.

C: I award an indirect free-kick to the opposition.

MURPHY

OSBORN   COLBACK

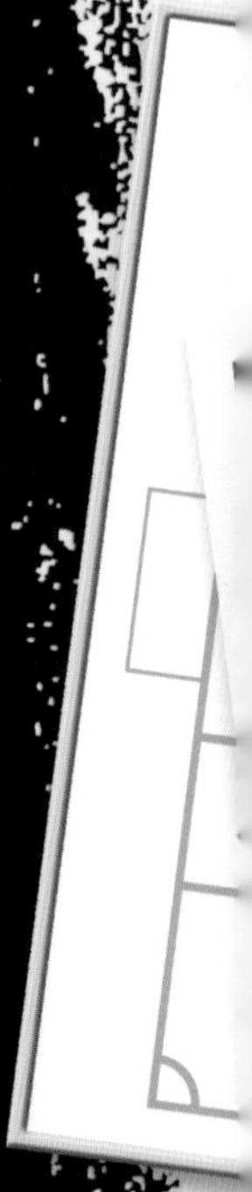

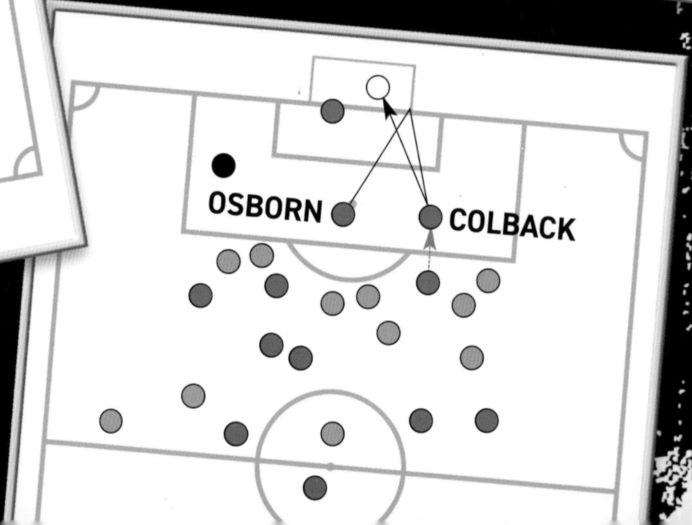

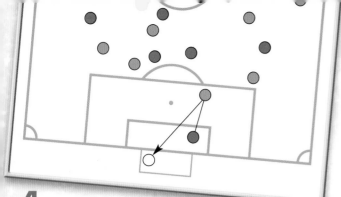

4. After another Forest attack goes close, the opposing keeper attempts to take a quick goal kick, but to his horror, the ball hits his right-back who is still in the penalty area and deflects into his own net. What's your call?

A: It's a goal!

B: A corner kick to Forest.

C: The goal kick has to be retaken.

5. Standing in his own penalty area, Luke Steele catches the ball directly from teammate Liam Bridcutt's throw-in. What's your decision?

A: Everything's fine. Play on.

B: You award the opposing team an indirect free-kick.

C: A yellow card for Steele and a penalty for the opposing team.

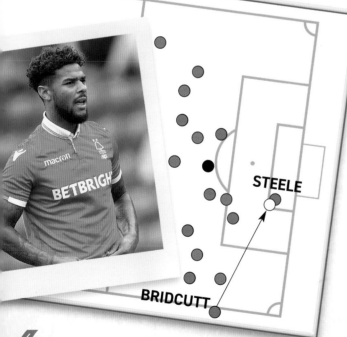

6. You have decided Matty Cash's spot kick must be re-taken after an infringement by the keeper. This time Ben Osborn steps forward to take the kick. Is that allowed?

A: No, I award an indirect free kick to the opposition.

B: Yes, any City player can re-take the penalty.

C: No, the player who took the initial spot kick, Matty Cash, must retake the kick.

7. You award a drop ball. As you drop the ball, Jack Colback and the opposing player both kick the ball at the same time before it hits the turf. What's your ruling?

A: You show a yellow card to both players for ungentlemanly conduct.

B: You drop the ball again.

C: Play on.

8. Lewis Grabban is on the scoresheet again, tapping in from only three yards out. When he scores, he is slightly ahead of the last defender, but in line with the goalkeeper. What is your decision?

A: Goal. in line with the keeper is not offside.

B: Goal disallowed. Grabban is offside. To be onside, he must be in line with the second last opponent or the ball.

C: Goal. A player can't be offside inside the six-yard box.

9. Matty Cash takes a long throw in aiming for the head of Michael Dawson. No-one makes contact with the ball and it bounces into the net direct from Cash's throw. What's your call, ref?

A: Goal. Providing there was an attempt to play the ball.

B: Goal. As long as the throw-in was taken correctly.

C: No Goal. A goal can never be scored direct from a throw in.

FOREST ANSWERS

PAGE 26 · FAN'TASTIC
Trevor Francis, Tony Woodcock, Kevin Campbell, Des Walker and Stuart Pearce.

PAGE 34 · GUESS THE CLUB
1. Ajax. 2. Paris Saint-Germain. 3. Bayern Munich.
4. Sporting Lisbon. 5. Real Madrid. 6. Arsenal. 7. Celtic.
8. Juventus. 9. Barcelona. 10. Club Brugge.

PAGE 40 · WHO ARE YER?
1. Jack Robinson. 2. Jack Colback. 3. Costel Pantilimon.
4. Diogo Goncalves. 5. Gil Dias. 6. Jack Robinson.
7. Adlene Guedioura. 8. Tobias Figueiredo.

PAGE 43 · SPOT THE DIFFERENCE

PAGE 45 · 2017/18 END OF TERM EXAM
1. Barrie McKay. 2. 3-2. 3. Kieran Dowell, 9. 4. QPR 2-5 Forest.
5. 13. 6. Ben Osborn. 7. Millwall. 8. Liam Bridcutt, 11.
9. Barrie McKay and Eric Lichaj. 10. 51.

PAGE 53 · SPOT THE BALL

PAGE 53 · WHAT BALL?
Ball D.

PAGE 56 · HERO HUNT
Trevor Francis.

PAGE 57 · SHIRT SHUFFLE
1. Liverpool. 2. Fulham. 3. Sheffield United. 4. Birmingham City.
5. West Ham United. 6. Crystal Palace. 7. Bournemouth.
8. Queens Park Rangers. 9. Stoke City. 10. Newcastle United.
11. Preston North End. 12. Aston Villa

PAGE 60 · HEY REF!
1. B. 2. C. 3. A. 4. C. 5. B. 6. B. 7. B. 8. B. 9. C.